Dad & Daughter Forever Bond

Written and Illustrated by
Jonathan Hill

Get Free Color by Number book send a Mail
After Purchase to info@harbourhousepress.co.uk

Dedicated to my Kids:
Val, Vishal and Videl

H O U S E P U B L I S H I N G L T D

This Book
Belongs to

_____

_____

When you need someone to talk to, a shoulder to cry on, or just a listening ear, know that I am always here, ready to support you, comfort you, and wipe away your tears.

When the world seems scary and big, I'll hold your hand and be your guide, showing you the beauty in every corner and giving you the courage to reach for the sky.

When you achieve your dreams and accomplishments, I'll be your biggest cheerleader, celebrating your successes, and reminding you that your hard work and dedication paid off.

When you need a break from the hustle and bustle of life, I'll take you on adventures, create memories with you, and show you that the world is full of wonders and beauty.

When you have doubts about yourself, I'll be your mirror, reflecting back all the wonderful qualities that make you unique, special, and loved.

When you make mistakes and fall down, I'll be your safety net, catching you and helping you get back up, teaching you that failure is just another step on the journey to success.

When you're feeling lost or confused, I'll be your compass, helping you find your way and guiding you towards your true purpose and passion.

When you're happy and joyful, I'll share in your joy, laughing with you, dancing with you, and reminding you that happiness is contagious and should be spread around.

When you grow up
and start your own
family, I'll still be there,
supporting you and
loving you, always
proud to be your dad
and grateful for the
bond we share.

When you need a role model, I'll be your guide, showing you how to live with integrity, kindness, and compassion, and being an example of what a good person should be.

When you feel alone or isolated, I'll be your friend, listening to your stories, sharing in your passions, and being there to remind you that you are loved and appreciated.

When you face the world and its challenges, I'll be your shield, protecting you from harm and danger, and giving you the courage and strength to face anything that comes your way.

When you need advice or guidance, I'll be your wise elder, offering you insights and perspectives that come from a lifetime of experience, and helping you make the best decisions for yourself.

When you need a hug or a cuddle, I'll be your comforter, holding you close and giving you the warmth and security that only a father's embrace can provide.

When you have questions about life, love, or anything else, I'll be your guru, sharing with you the knowledge and wisdom that I have gained over the years, and helping you find the answers you seek.

When you grow up and become a woman, I'll still see you as my little girl, always holding a special place in my heart, and forever grateful for the joy and love you bring into my life.